THE WONDERFUL WORL

MALDIVES

BONECHI

Distributed by:

Sun Front Pvt. Ltd.

Malè, Republic of Maldives.
Tel: 960 323467, Fax 960 323466
e-mail: admin@sunfront.com.mv
Internet: www.sunfront.com.mv

INTRODUCTION

"Maldives": the name alone has the power to evoke the picture of an extraordinarily enchanting and uncontaminated island setting and it has thus become synonymous for the ideal dream holiday, free from the limits of conditioning and the stress produced by the feverish rhythm of modern life. This fame really does seem to be justified even if we simply leaf through brochures at a travel agents, and it is fully confirmed in videos and in the accounts of those fortunate people who have been able to enjoy a holiday there.

As they are islands, and moreover, tropical ones, the image of the Maldives which comes to mind even without the help of documentary pictures is that of great white sand beaches, bordered by tall slender palms, which are mirrored in the extraordinarily warm, clear and calm water. On the horizon the crystalline blue of the sea merges with the cerulean blue of the sky, whilst the scarse human presence on the shore line (in striking difference to the oppressive overcrowding along our coasts) contrasts with the veritable explosion of colours and of vegetal and animal life on the sea bottom, populated by a phantasmagoria of algae, corals, molluscs and other forms of aquatic life. Unlike other holiday itineraries, both personalised and tourist, which in reality may turn out to be misleading and disappointing, the Maldives do not fail to fulfil the expectations of visitors and appear to correspond fully to the seemingly fantastic and idyllic picture sketched beforehand. Even more than one might imagine, the constant presence of the sea remains the dominant feature in the landscape, due, above all, to the small size of the islands of the archipelago: in fact, no place in the Maldives lies further than a few kilometres from the sea even on the larger islands. In addition to this, in this universe of rocks, shoals and little islands which make up the various atolls, there are no hills or other kinds of altimetric morphology which could in some way limit the view.

The importance of the sea is also apparent if we take a superficial look at a map, or better still at a planisphere: the Maldives are located in the central part of the Indian Ocean and are a few hundred kilometres from the nearest coastal state (India): in the great subdivision of islands into continental and oceanic they therefore have every right to be placed within the second category. Despite the fact that their insular character is therefore largely dominant, the Maldives have almost never suffered from excessive isolation as they are located along the

The sea of the Maldives seen from the shade of coconut palms on Kuramathi, one of the islands in the Rashdoo Atoll.

The golden dome of the Centre for Islamic Studies, at Malé.

principal traffic routes between Europe, Africa and the Middle East on one side and the Indian subcontinent, the Far East and Australia on the other. Thus it is not by chance that evidence exists showing that they were already populated in the IV-V century B.C. However, a series of legends and scientific theories, partly born out by archaeological finds, even advance the hypothesis of the presence of inhabitants at least a millennium before. Written accounts, which thus are certainly reliable, by Pappo of Alexandria and Scolastico of Thebes, and in the VI century A.D. by another Alexandrian, Cosma Indicopleuste, show the islands were already known in the IV century B.C.

The first colonizers of the island almost certainly came from what is now Sri Lanka or from Southern India and were probably of Aryan stock. The mythical Koimala, who having landed on the islands was proclaimed king by the natives, was also of this race. From the very remote past until fairly recent times their religion was Buddism, as is confirmed by the various remains of temples and pagodas, for example those of the atoll of Ari. Conversion to the Islamic religion dates back to 1153 and was performed by one of the many Arab merchants who travelled the route from the East to India: the Berber Abu-al-Bakarat. He dared to challenge one of the terrible sea demons worshiped on the islands (Jinis), preventing, by praying, the sacrifice of a virgin who was intended to placate the anger of the monster. The whole population, filled with admiration at this feat, was converted to Islamism and their chief became the first sultan of the Maldives. The modest tomb of the Arab merchant (Medu Ziyaarath) *in the presidential garden of Malé is still a sacred place.*

Three great dynasties succeeded one another on the throne of the archipelago until the Portuguese arrived and in 1558 managed to subjugate the islands under the leadership of Captain Andreas Andre (in Maldivian Andhiri Andhirin) and to kill Sultan Alì the Martyr. There were various attempts at rebellion during the Portuguese occupation, which was particularly hard and violent, and they finally had a positive outcome due to the heroic exploits of the three Thakurufaan brothers. Although the eldest was captured and executed, the other two carried out a sort of guerrilla warfare which forced the invaders to surrender, allowing Mohammed Thakurufaan to be crowned as sultan. The Maldives continued, however, to be a target for foreign powers: after various further attempts to land on the part of the Portuguese, the islands were sacked several times by the Moplas pirates who had their bases on the Indian coast of Malabar. The invaders were repelled thanks to the heroism of certain chiefs (prominent among whom were Ibrahim Iskandar I, who constructed various minarets and the mosque of Malé, and Ghazee Hassan Izzuddeen), but eventually the sultans of the archipelago considered it wiser to place themselves under the protection of first the French, then the Dutch of Ceylon, and finally of the

English, after they had taken possession of the large island nearby. Right back in 1887, and then again in 1948, the English recognised the full independence of the Maldives, although they shouldered the burden of their defense in exchange for substantial economic benefits and the concession of a aeronaval base on the island of Addu. In modern times the most important historical events for the islands were the agreement with Great Britain which established total independence (signed in 1965), the admission to the United Nations after a few months, the transformation of the sultanate into a presidential republic (1968) and the end of the English presence at the aeronaval base on Gan (1976).

The Maldives are now, therefore, a presidential republic, provided with a parliament which has legislative powers (Majlis), *which stays in office for five years and is elected on a territorial basis by the 19 atolls which make up the basic administrative units. The population amounts to about 270,000 inhabitants, a quarter of whom live in the capital Malé. They are largely of Sinhalese origin, but their primitive somatic characteristics have become much less distinct during centuries of contacts with the Arab and African world: their chief characteristic is low stature which makes them easy to distinguish from the Indians of more recent immigration. A psychological and sociological profile would reveal a very simple and peaceable disposition, and normally they also appear to be blessed with extreme good spirits and scarse aggressiveness. With a pinch of irony and malice, this natural predisposition towards optimism and cheerfulness can perhaps be explained at least in part by the simple fact of a very widespread custom in the Maldives, that of legally ending conjugal relations which do not work with extreme ease, thus putting an end to many reasons for argument and worry. Given the extreme simplicity of the legal action (it is only necessary to say three times in quick succession "I divorce you" before a public official, called a* gazi, *who will draw up the act), the frequency of divorce is very striking, so much so that some people manage to perform this act up to twenty times in their lives. In spite of this, the character of the islanders is all in all particularly romantic, as is testified by their great love for music and poetry, which is expressed in particular in choral singing, dancing, ballads, verse and prose. This artistic and poetic entertainment tends to exalt, above all, love for nature and its deep harmony, and an efficient instrument of expression is found in the notable level of elaboration which has been reached both in the written and the spoken language. The spoken language* (Dhivehi) *derives from the aggregation of Arabic, Indian and English words into the primitive sinhala language (Sinhalese) and thus it has a very rich and expressive vocabulary. The written language* (Thaana) *was introduced in the XVI century by the legendary hero Thakurufaan and is made up of 24 letters, which are*

A view of the white sandy beaches of Ihuru on North Malé Atoll.

graphically similar to those of the Arabic and Persian alphabets, but are, all in all, simpler: its evident Arabic origin also shows clearly in the fact that it is read from right to left.
From the preceding short historical summary, and in particular regarding the martial events, the extremely important strategic role of the Maldives stands out clearly. In recent times they have even been described as the "aircraft-carriers of the Indian Ocean" and have whetted the appetites of the greatest world powers (Great Britain, United States, Soviet Union, China). From this point of view, their capacity to maintain relative political and administrative autonomy appears quite extraordinary, if one considers the enormous dispersion of the archipelago and the exceptional number of islands of which it is made up: we are talking, in fact, of about 1192 officially recognised islands (of which little more than 200 are permanently lived on) , but their number rises to over two thousand if one counts the minor cays. The dimensions of the islands are, in fact, generally very small, a fact which can clearly be seen from the total surface area of the whole archipelago: just 298 square kilometres of land, more or less the surface area of the Tuscan archipelago. This myriad of rocks and small islands is furthermore spread out in a vast area (almost 90,000 sq.km.) which extends for over 800 kilometres in a latitudinal direction and 130 in a longitudinal direction, giving rise to a long island axis, positioned in a North-South direction. The very name "Maldives," however much it is of debatable interpretation, seems to refer to the morphologic layout of the archipelago or to the very large number of islands of which it is composed, deriving from the Sanskrit malodheep *(garland) or* mal dvipa *(a thousand islands).*
Both the unusual arrangement of the islands and the extraordinary quantity of them are directly attributable to the very origin of the archipelago, largely linked to the action of coral-producing polyps. In fact, these are coral reefs and islands which have developed for the most part in the characteristic atoll structure: even this word, which as is known, indicates a typical ring arrangement of the coastline, comes, not by chance, from a word of Maldivian origin (atholhu). *In the Maldives almost all the land above sea-level is, in fact, positioned in a garland around the 26 main atolls which make up the archipelago and bound inner basins of wonderfully calm, transparent and crystalline water. The temperature of the water, generally higher than that of the surrounding ocean (by virtue of the strong irradiation of the sun on the shallows of the lagoon), favours the presence of luxuriant and exuberant underwater flora and fauna.*
Much has been written about the origin of the atolls, but the most credible theory remains that of the

The sea around the Maldives has an ideal temperature for a vast variety of marine species; this also makes it very popular with divers.

A group of divers preparing for immersion at Halaveli, Alifu Atoll.

great naturalist and geographer Charles Darwin who guessed that the ring-shaped arrangement of the madreporic reefs was probably due to the gradual submersion of a pre-existing island, often of volcanic origin, either due to it sinking, or due to sea levels rising during the present interglacial period: the development of coral-producing colonies, in fact, can only take place in moderate depths where the presence of dissolved oxygen and of sunlight are greater, for which reason the polyps were obliged to progressively raise their constructions along the old perimeter of the submerged island. Contrary to common belief, however, the colonies of polyps only provide the frame of barrier reefs, whilst a large part of the organogenic calcareous rock which makes them up (about 90%) derives from other marine organisms, for example alghe and molluscs, which find protection in the gorges of the reef. The action of sea and wind then deposit large quantities of debris on the submerged madreporic reefs until they completely emerge and the growth of pioneer surface vegetation starts. These sands, also of organic origin, are generally very white and they also settle along the sides of the lagoon, giving rise to the magnificent beaches which characterise madreporic islands. In many cases the calcareous ring of which the atoll is made up is discontinuous, which makes the coastal setting even more magical and allows boats and open-sea fish to enter the inner lagoons.

Precisely because of this particular morphological origin, because of the lack of hills to shelter them from the wind and because of their position in the middle of the open ocean, the Maldives would seem to be particularly exposed to the risk of hurricanes and cyclones, which are frequent in other subequatorial and tropical areas. This risk is however only seeming, in that the climate appears conditioned by the presence of the monsoon wind which blows periodically from or towards the continent. In winter the earth monsoon from the north-east prevails; it is dry and relatively cool, and brings clear skies from December to April. In the summer, on the other hand, the sea monsoon arrives, blowing from the south-west and loaded with humidity derived from the evaporation of the ocean; it brings rainy and unsettled weather from May to October. The absence of hills, which would cause the cloud mass passing over on its way to the Indian subcontinent to rise and instantaneously discharge its water content, limits the quantity (about 2000 mm of rain per annum) and above all the violence of rainfall. It is for this reason that even in the more humid period the rains do not arrive with the devastating violence with which they usually hit the not far away coasts of Bengal, Malabar and Coromandel. Sea storms, which may take place above all during the change of season linked to the inversion of the monsoon, are furthermore kept under control by the natural defense provided by the coral reefs, which limit the

force of the waves in the inner lagoons.
Generally speaking the climate of the Maldives can be described as hot and humid, with average air temperatures which oscillate between 26 and 33°C. The heat is, however, mitigated by the presence of gentle and constant sea breezes which make staying here very pleasant for tourists. The same can be said for the sea water which, in addition to its already much-praised qualities of transparency, limpidity and colour, has a temperature which never goes below 24°C and thus allows the presence of a very rich underwater life.
Despite the quite high air and water temperatures which are constant throughout the year, the coral islands which make up the archipelago of the Maldives only have luxuriant vegetation in some places: the scarcity of vegetal soil and the lack of fresh water, both surface (rivers and lakes) and underground (springs), along with their small size (most of the islands measure less than a square kilometre surface area) and the very nature of the coral reefs of the islands, greatly limit the growth of large and flourishing plants and trees; however, the magnificent coconut palms which border the lagoons, some areas of rain forest (from which fine wood is obtained) and the mangroves are an exception. The cultivated areas are not very extensive and are unable to provide even the basic food necessities for the inhabitants: for this reason, and to supply the high demand for foodstuffs occasioned by the development of tourism, large quantities of agricultural produce, particularly rice, are imported from other countries. Despite this, all the islands which are inhabited all year round have, of course, small plantations for the sustenance of the local population, where grains (above all millet, maize and sorghum), tuberous plants (cassava, taro and sweet potato), flour plants (bread-fruit tree), vegetables (particularly onions and peppers) and fruit (bananas, mangoes, papayas, pineapples and other typical tropical fruit largely destined for tourist consumption) are cultivated. But the principal agricultural resource of the Maldives is still the coconut palm, which probably originated on these very islands, and which even grows spontaneously from the fruit which falls to the ground from the parent tree. It is not by chance that the coconut palm appears in the Maldives' national coat of arms and that it is explicitly described as "Dhivehi ruh," *which means the palm of the Maldives. The economical and cultural importance of the coconut, after all, goes much further than the simple production of the fruit (which, however, are also exported). It plays an important characterising role in the traditional and particular life style of the islanders: in other words, for the people of the Maldives the coconut palm has an importance comparable with that of the bison for the Red Indians of the Great Plains in America or the reindeer for the Laplanders. It supplies a part of their food, oil and copra, wood for houses and boats, leaves to make*

A school of "Powder Blue Tangs" (Acanthurus leucosternon) in the waters of the Maldives.

Malé: fishermen unloading the catch.
Fishing has always been the main economic activity of the country.

mats and vegetal roofing, the fibres for ropes and fabrics and even a strong non-alcoholic drink "Toddy". *It is not without reason that the rent of an island is still established on the basis of the number of palms on it. However, for centuries the main economic activity in the Maldives has been fishing and it has only recently been undermined by the development of tourism. The Indian Ocean as a whole has over 700 species of fish most of which are present in the waters of the Maldives, which can for this reason be likened to a real natural aquarium: the shallows of the archipelago are populated by thousands of marine organisms with extraordinary colours, and of all shapes and sizes, giving the impression of a underwater paradise. This abundance of fish, favoured by the presence of relatively warm and shallow water, well oxygenated by the currents, has been exploited by the island population for centuries; their economy and their life-style have been built on fishing. More than a fifth of island labour is still employed in the fishing sector today and from this sector a sixth of the entire gross national product is obtained. Even in the remote past, however, the catch was smoked or dried in the sun and exported to the coasts of India and the now Sri Lanka, under the name of "fish from the Maldives". Today fishing still largely takes place in the traditional boats hollowed out of coconut palm wood, called "dhoni", which carry 8-10 fishermen headed by a boat leader* (keolu). *For this reason, above all at dawn and sunset, the sea of the Maldives appears to be full of dozens of little sail'boats and rowing boats which make the coastal panorama even more enchanting. Even today the fishing techniques normally used are, in fact, still the traditional ones (fishing-lines and small nets), even though the government is trying to modernise both the production systems and the means employed. In order to avoid competition with the states nearby and particularly those with more advanced technology (above all Japan), the territorial waters have been extended by unilateral measures to 200 miles from the coast. This drastic measure to protect the ocean's fish in general and the archipelago's shoals of fish in particular, has been accompanied by the construction of modern plants for the preservation of fish which, today is exported mostly salted, frozen and tinned to the countries of the Far East (Japan, Korea, Singapore) and to Europe. The largest and most important catches from an economic point of view are mackerel and, above all, bonito, a type of small tuna fish which, once it is smoked and salted, is not only a nutritious and appetizing food, but is believed by the islanders to possess great strengthening and stimulating powers, to the extent of instilling exceptional physical energy and strength in whoever eats it.*
The Maldives sea also provided, at least up to the sixteenth century, another basic resource from an

economic point of view. This was the shells of the Cyprea moneta *variety which due to their beauty and as their name states, were for centuries the principal currency for trade on the Asiatic and African coasts of the Indian Ocean. The official foreign currency of the state became the rufiya a long time ago, but the shells which made the Maldives known as the ancient "money islands" are still collected by the natives to make necklaces and souvenirs.*

As far as the other economic activities are concerned it is worth noting that within the secondary sectors modern-type industries have in some cases taken the place of the old traditional craftsmen: for example, in the field of the construction of fibre glass pleasure craft and in that of the preservation of fish. Numerous forms of artisan production still remain, however, for example the production of ropes, wooden and metal objects and utensils, fishing boats in coconut palm wood and even the building of the very houses, constructed in palm wood on foundations of blocks of calcareous rock, hewn with an axe from the coral-reefs. The typical local handicrafts, which are mostly produced by women, appear to be largely destined for the tourist market and consist above all of coral, mother-of-pearl, and shell necklaces, objects made of varnished wood, coconut fibre carpets and mats, embroidery and arabesques.

The main source of income is now tourism which can count on about 200,000 visitors yearly, by far the largest part of whom stay in the seventy or so hotel structures spread out on the main islands: in order to prevent an excessive impact on the environment and to limit the spread of modern and exclusive establishments (private clubs, residences, etc.), the government has set extremely severe taxes on building these on the islands which are not permanently lived on. It is worth mentioning that the discovery and the widespread tourist enjoyment of the naturalistic treasures of the Maldives was largely the work of Italians. Even now Italian tourists are a fifth of the total number, preceded only by Germans (almost a quarter), and European tourists taken all together are abundantly predominant. In addition to the extraordinary beauty of the natural surroundings and a notable series of good quality reception structures, tourists can also count on a rich programme of cultural and folkloric entertainment, which have their origin largely in Islamic tradition or in pre-existing tribal beliefs of an animistic type: even now, for example, fear of demons and monsters is particularly strong and thus they are exorcized by special witch-doctors (hakeem) *using rites, antidotes and potions. The society of the Maldives is nevertheless pretty pervaded by the Sunnite Muslim culture, strongly present in schools, religion and politics and in the usages of daily life: the very Constitution defines the Republic of the Maldives as Islamic and the national flag clearly shows a white Crescent on a green background, bordered with red. Precisely because it is the state religion, Islamism has a fundamental role in the Maldives, and is present everywhere, even if it has particularly liberal attitudes and characteristics and is directed towards tolerance: nobody questions the daily prayers, the Ramadan celebrations and the Koranic law, but the women are, for example, exempt from wearing veils to cover their faces. From an strictly folkloric point of view the folk dances in costume, accompanied by traditional music mostly performed on percussion instruments as in the* "bodu beru," *in the* "thaara,"*or in the* "kadhaa maali" *are particularly fascinating for tourists.*

A splendid example of the hibiscus, a flowering plant found on many of the islands, and a typical Maldives sunset.

Mangroves, plants with prop root systems, are not uncommon in the Maldives.

belair

MALÉ

If in western tourist iconography the Maldives are a typical equatorial "dream," where commonplaces about the paradisial, virtually primordial, nature and surroundings are "dished out" without any sort of limitation, it is at any rate true that the first approach to these fairy-tale islands is an experience which is not easily forgotten. The first contact that the tourist has with the archipelago of the Maldives takes place, of necessity, from the porthole of an aeroplane on its way to the International Airport of Malé. Then before there is time to get over the intoxicating sensation given by the sight of the coral atolls emerging from the abyssal depths of the Indian Ocean, with their play of colours, reflections, transparency and nuances at the bounds of reality, the descent starts towards a tiny tongue of land, elongated and narrow, surrounded by the sea and emerging from the coral reef. The island of Hulhule is the umbilical cord linking the Maldives with the rest of the world: the airport there was re-opened after expansion in 1981 and since then it has received steadily growing numbers of visitors (charter connections from Europe, Egypt and Taiwan; regular airline company connections with the most varied destinations). In fact, there has been an increase from 1097 aeroplanes in 1972 to the 221,000 recorded at the end of 1991. It takes a few minutes to reach Malé by boat from the airport, or, alternatively, transport to one of the other tourist destinations of the archipelago is available.

What may be described as the smallest capital in the world, is two and a half kilometres long and one kilometre wide. It is located on the atoll of Malé (*Kaafu Atoll*), which is situated in a median position in relation to the archipelago, which extends vertically north of the Equator. The island, which is the political, cultural and economic centre, has more than 55,000 residents, as well as a large number of commuters from the other islands of the Maldives, who go there to benefit from the services (commerce, health service education) which make Malé into a real pole of attraction as well as a "capital" as it is usually understood.

Not far from *Marina Drive*, the sea-front which en-

A plane on the runway of the Malé International Airport on the island of Hulhule, just a few kilometers from the nation's capital, and vessels coming to berth in the harbor.

The modern Malé skyline from the sea.

Malé: the elegant and modern architectural lines of the Islamic Centre.

Malé: a charming picture of the golden cupola and the minaret of the Great Mosque in the Islamic Centre.

Malé: the unusual cylindrical structure of the Minaret calls the Muslims to their ritual prayers.

circles the island for a very large proportion of its perimeter (and on to which face various important government offices and the travel agents), rises the **Islamic Centre**. Its golden cupola (actually made out of anodised aluminium) sets its mark on the skyline of Malé along with the attached **Minaret** (*Munnaaru*), which is visible from afar (particularly well from the boat which brings the tourists visiting the island). This three-storey building was inaugurated in 1984. It was built with the help of Brunei, Malaysia and Pakistan and includes the **Great Mosque**, which has been named after Sultan Thakurufaanu Al A'z'am. A visit

Malé: a view of Medhu Ziyaarath, the Mausoleum of Abul Barakaat, who converted the Maldives to Islamism.

Malé: the portal of the Mausoleum of Abul Barakaat.

to this Islamic place of worship is certainly interesting, but one must not, however, forget the duties of a guest in a Muslim country. Therefore, scanty and untidy dress should be avoided and one must remember to take off one's shoes and submit willingly to the ritual of the ablution of the feet in one of the lustral fountains provided for this purpose. In return one can admire the great Prayer Hall, big enough to hold almost 6000 believers and decorated with wood carvings of good workmanship and inscriptions in Arabic.

Not far from this centre of obvious cultural and religious significance rises the **Presidential Palace** (*Mulee-Aage*). The present-day native name for the palace refers to that of a building already in existence half-way through the XVII century. The residence was for a long time the dwelling of the Manikufaan, a family of which the most famous member was Muleege Dhon Hassan Manikufaan, who is a national hero of the Maldives for having repulsed an attack by the pirates of Malabar (now Kerala) and thus restoring independence to the archipelago. He became sultan with the title Hassan

Malé: a partial view of the Presidential Palace.

A rounded tombstone indicates the burial-place of a woman, whereas a pointed one represents that of a man.

Izzudhdheen and reigned from 1759 to 1767. After his death the palace became the official residence of his descendants. But the more recent history of the presidential building dates from 1906, when Sultan Mhamed Shamsudhdheen III had the palace which we see today built for his heir, Al-Ameer Hassan Izzudhdheen. This building, named *Henveyru Ganduvaru*, was constructed by the Maldivians themselves, with the aid of architects from Ceylon (Sri Lanka), co-ordinated by Al-Ameer Ahmed Kuda Doshimeynaa Kilegefaan. Rather than Muslim architecture in the strict sense of the word, the Presidential Palace gives a decidedly foreign impression, which for westerners brings to mind various characteristics present in Disneyland buildings, or at any rate, certain typically American constructions. When the Sultan and his family were exiled to an island of a far off atoll of the archipelago (1936), the palace came under government administration, undergoing restoration, reconstruction and taking the name *Mulee-Aage*. Already the seat of important offices and institutions, it became the presidential residence on 1-1-1953, the date which marks the institutional

Malé: the Hukuru Miskiiy Mosque and a detail of the cemetery.

transformation of the Maldives from Sultanate to Republic.
An unusual building surrounded by numerous white flags is to be found in the vicinity; this is the **Medhu Ziyaarath**, the mausoleum of Abul Barakaat Yoosuf Al Barbary, a Moroccan who "exported" Islamic religion to the Maldives (1153).
Another unusual note in the picturesque town centre of Malé is struck by the **Minaret** (*Munnaaru*), a squat cylindrical construction (1675), on the top of which loudspeakers call the faithful to prayer, substituting the legendary figure of the muezzin.
The nearby **Cemetery** presents a completely different picture from that which a Western visitor

The new President's Palace and a lively street in Malé.

would expect to find: rather than a cemetery, it is a garden shaded by luxuriant coconut palms, to which the white shape of the minaret, beautifully inscribed in Islamic with descriptions of historical scenes, provides a striking wing. The bright white of this construction, often set against an extraordinarily deep blue sky, seems to be reflected by the numerous tomb stones protruding from the ground. These are covered with Arabic epigraphs and they end in a point if the dead person was male whereas they are rounded on top if the corpse buried below was female.
Looking round this secluded and evocative place, one is struck by the **Hukuru Miskiiy**, a mosque in coral stone built in the second half of the XVII century, at the time of Sultan Ibrahim Iskandhar. A roofing-over made of iron panels protects the building from the harmful rays of the sun. The inside is rich in Arabic epigraphs which testify the conversion of the islands to the Islamic faith. The tombs of various sovereigns, notables and heroes of this

The long straightaway of Malé's "Marina Drive."

On this and the next page, images of the gaily colored fishermen's boats docked in the island's fishing port.

far away island world stand out amongst the numerous tombs here.
Quite apart from aspects of tourist interest in the more strict sense, Malé generally offers a charming scenic picture, composed and orderly in its own way, with a sea front road (*Marina Drive*) which covers three sides of the island, the form of which is, more or less, rectangular. The low houses fit into green surroundings where trees and plants abound, surrounded by the sea, which is life and work at the same time for this island people for whom fishing is one of the main economic activities. Wherever one looks one sees boats of various kinds and sizes. Some are used for transporting tourists and to connect this island with the other atolls, but they are often much more simply the age-old link, established between man and the sea right from the beginnings of civilisation.

Daily life in Malé, a city in continual evolution, a blend of tradition and innovation. A typical local market, a picturesque street enlivened by the colors of the flowers and the deep green of the palms and other trees, the seafront boulevard with a parking facility for bicycles (a common and convenient means of transport on this relatively small island), and a hand-drawn fish cart, still a valid alternative to motorized carriers.

VENEELA

Aspects of the Malé marina: various types of craft alternate with the characteristic Maldivian fishing boats, whilst all around the hectic activity of the fishermen can be seen.

These photographs, and those which follow, document the maritime character of the Maldives clearly: a paradisiacal island country which, however, requires hard daily labour from its inhabitants, in order to procure their means of sustenance.

More pictures which show the vitality of fishing as a leading sector stimulating the economy of the Maldives. Even if it is also true that in the last few years a role which certainly cannot be disregarded in the economic growth of the archipelago was played by tourism, it must be noted that fishing is still, even today, a primary source of income for the Maldivians. The waters of the ocean, abounding in fish, contain tuna, mackerel and barracuda; characteristic are the "Blue Marvin", a typical species of the archipelago and the so-called "Maldives fish", a type of dried and smoked tuna-fish, largely destined for export (Sri Lanka). Despite the rationalization of the systems of processing, storing and preservation of fish, combined with the motorization of the boats, many islanders still use the characteristic dhoni (the typical Maldivian sailboat) to fish in the ocean.
These pictures show us the fish market, which is held in this two-storey building, and demonstrate the hectic activity of the fishermen of Malé, busy with the fish they have just caught.

On these pages, some aspects of the more modern side of Malé: a lovely rectangular space for open-air shows, the meeting center, a residential district, and the futuristic forms of another building.
The alternation of ancient buildings and contemporary architecture in Malé reflects a process of constant development that often gives the impression that the city never ceases to change.

General Information

Flag

The national flag of the Maldives is red, green, and white: a rectangle of green, alluding to the palms, the life source of the islands, is surrounded by a red ground, representing the sacrifice of the national heroes; at the center is the white crescent moon, symbol of the Muslim religion.

Religion

The official religion of the Maldives is Islam. Prayer (five times every day) takes precedence over all other activities so that even business and recreation are suspended by the cry of the 'muezzin'.

The Language

'Dhivehi' is spoken throughout the archipelago. The roots of this tongue reach into the ancient languages of southern Asia with an admixture of Arabic and Hindi and some English words.
English is spoken in a great number of the resorts, but French, German, and Italian are also widely used.
The written language, which uses Arabic characters and proceeds from right to left, is 'Thaana'.

The Currency

The 'Rufiyaa' and the 'Laaree' are the basic units of Maldivian currency. 100 'Laarees' equal 1 'Rufiyaa'.
The bills are 2, 5, 10, 20, 50, 100, and 500 'Rufiyaas'; coins are 1 and 2 'Rufiyaas' and 50, 20, 10, 5, 2, and 1 'Laarees'.

The National Tree

The national tree of the Maldives is the beneficent coconut palm, every part of which can be used—and in fact is. From the delicious fruits (obviously) to the fronds, which are plaited to create roofing material and brooms (but also baskets and trays), to the branches, which are carved to create artistic crafts items.

The National Emblem

The national emblem of the Maldives is the crescent moon, a star, two national flags, and a banner with the traditional name of the country: Ad Dawlat Al Mahaldheebiyya.

The Islanders

The population of the Maldives is about 270,000, one-third of whom live in the capital city of Malé. About 20,000 foreign workers are employed in the tourist sector: the majority is Sinhalese, but there are also many Indians and Europeans.

The National Flower

In 1985, the pink rose was chosen as the only flower suitable for representing the singular beauty of the country.

Island Administration

The twenty-six "geographic" atolls are apportioned into twenty "administrative" atolls. Each Island Chief ('Katheeb') reports to an Atoll Chief ('Atholhuverin') and all are responsible to the central government.

LIFE IN THE MALDIVES

Most of the permanent inhabitants of the Maldives do not make their homes on the "tourist" islands (that is, those islands entirely occupied by the luxurious resorts), but instead live in the capital and on certain other islands of the various atolls. These so-called "fishermen's islands" are thus the focus of the hustle and bustle that characterizes the daily lives of the Maldivians, and it is here that the basic characteristics of life in the archipelago emerge most clearly.

The day's activities begin early, right after the first, predawn prayer between 4:30 and 5:00 in the morning. Afterwards, the women fix breakfast and get the children ready for school, while the men go off to their places of work.

The main occupation of the inhabitants of the Maldives is fishing, as is only natural in a country so intimately linked to the sea.

The fishermen prepare their nets and set out on their dhonis before sunrise. When the boats return, generally before sunset, they are beset by a crowd of older people and children come to inspect the day's catch. The fish netted by each dhoni are divided equally between the owner of the boat and the crew; by tradition, any dhoni that has caught more than a thousand fish flies a flag.

The fish is then cleaned and taken home for dinner, which the women traditionally prepare. After dinner the men gather to chat at the homes of the "captains" of the dhonis.

Women play an important role in the Maldivian community. They enjoy the same rights as men, such as the right to conduct business and own property in their own names, and equal opportunities for education and employment. Married women retain their maiden names.

A characteristic Maldivian vessel stands out against the waters of the ocean.

On the following pages, Maldivian fishermen at their daily work.

03-1047

These pictures show some characteristic features of the Maldives. Here we are on the island of Omadhoo, in the atoll of Alifu, north of the administrative center Mahibadhoo. Like many other islands in the archipelago, this is not a tourist island in the usual sense of the term (that is, there are no tourist developments). However, it is very interesting culturally and ethnographically, since it allows one to directly examine the environment in which the natives live.
The island of Omadhoo is one of the large group of "fishermen's Islands." The photographs show fishing boats at anchor, two Maldivian women intent on their domestic chores (observe the coral masonry of which the rustic house is built), and the attractive smile of a Maldivian girl.
The Maldivians are practising Muslims; of a peaceful and mild temperament, they are very hospitable toward tourists. Howether, they expect tourists to respect their habits, customs and religious beliefs.

On the preceding pages, more scenes of daily life in the Maldives archipelago. The fishermen, with their small vessels, seem almost to defy the apparent calm of the ocean.

Some beautiful pictures of the women of Omadhoo occupied with their daily domestic tasks.
The bottom right photo shows the preparation of curry, the most important seasoning in Maldivian and Sri-Lankan cuisine.

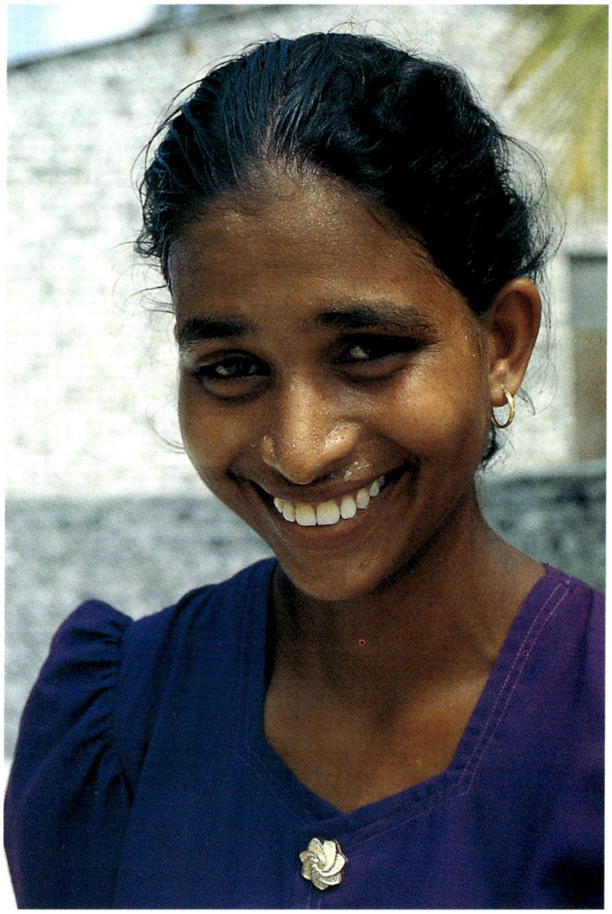

These pictures were taken on the island of Dhangethi, in the southern portion of the atoll of Alifu. Dhangethi is not a "tourist island"; however, like the many other "fishermen's islands," it has much to offer to the attentive eyes of western tourists. Here we see a close-up of a young Maldivian woman; the island seen from the landing stage, with a characteristic boat; shells, coral, sharks' teeth and a bit of everything displayed at the local market; and Maldivian women exhibiting their crafts wares in the opportune shade of coconut palms.

The lush vegetation of the island of Bandos, in the North Malé Atoll, and an example of Ixora Coccinea on Velassaru in the South Malé Atoll.

The so-called "Red Ginger" and another of the splendid flowers that enliven the Maldives with their magnificent colors.

true that many small islands host only a few shrubs or the typical coconut palm, by now the symbol of the "tropical paradise" par excellence, there are also small pockets of true rainforest on some of the larger islands.
Certain of the islands are used by the local population for growing edible plant crop plants: sweet potatoes and yams, watermelons, taro, and millet.
From this point of view, the most fertile of the islands is Fuamulaku, in the southernmost sector of the archipelago. It is home to a number of plantations, some of which cultivate such tropical fruits as mango and pineapple.

THE THRILL OF DIVING

The wealth of the variegated underwater world of the Maldives atolls is an unequaled attraction for diving enthusiasts. The waters of the archipelago conceal a multitude of diving sites, some of which rank very high on the world-class scale.
Many areas of the coral barrier reefs, with their incredible variety of underwater fauna in all the colors of the rainbow, are within easy reach of the islands. Thanks to the warmth of the water and visibility of up to 50 meters, even the most demanding dives are "comfortable" (not to mention unique) experiences.
All the island resorts offer their guests professional diving schools; the instructors hold courses for every proficiency level, from beginners to experts. In many cases, however, all that's needed is a mask and a snorkel to enjoy the incredible underwater panorama of the reefs, many of which are truly outstanding and just a short swim from the beach.
Some of the most beautiful sites, inhabited by rare species and often by species threatened with extinction, have been declared "protected marine areas"—but then, throughout the Maldives, paying maximum respect for a unique natural environment should be only common courtesy.
Some of the most interesting diving sites in the archipelago are the Maldive Victory Wreck near the island of Hulule, Banana Reef in the North Malé Atoll, Guraidhoo Corner in the South Malé Atoll, Shark Thila in the northern sector of the Alifu Atoll, and the Broken Rock site in southern Alifu.

An aerial view of the extraordinary waters off Thulusdhoo, in the North Malé Atoll.

Divers outfitting on the island of Viligilivaru in the Alifu Atoll.

Contrary to general opinion, diving is a sport for everyone that requires no special physical abilities.
Under the expert guidance of the highly-qualified instructors at the many diving centers, even people who have never dived before will quickly learn the basic techniques for safe, enjoyable diving with or without breathing equipment.
The diving centers offer expert divers the opportunity to perfect their skills and obtain specific diving certifications.
Diving enthusiasts will discover a wide range of services both at the resorts, where all the needed equipment is provided, and at sea, where diving assistance is often available.
On these pages, a group of tourists about to dive; on the facing page, the deck of a diving-support vessel with all the needed equipment.

THE UNDERWATER WORLD

It captures you at first glance with its shining play of magical shades of blue, green and turquoise: a crystal liquid which, like a jewelbox, conceals a universe which it is difficult to describe. It is a suspended world in which words like sound, dimension, and time lose their sense. Everything moves and is motionless at the same time: animals and plants dance in a single undulating rite which obeys a tremendous, irresistible and fascinating force.
The Maldives islands are oases of earthly paradise mounted like precious stones in rings of coral, madrepore and gorgonids. Diving only a few metres below the water allows the discovery of an unimaginable variety of fish that appear to have derived their colours from those of the rainbow: all around you dart schools of "*mushi mas,*" opening their ranks at your passing, parrotfish (which feed on coral and produce coralline sand), trumpetfish, surgeonfish, emperorfish, butterflyfish . . .
Every form of marine life is represented here, from the tiny dinoflagellantes to the magnificent and powerful whale shark, a creature which despite its impressive size feeds solely on plankton and is quite harmless. This is yet another illustration of the fact that in order to understand the intimate essence of nature one must go beyond mere appearances. Even the grey shark, a terrifying creature to look at, abandons with great difficulty its indifference to anything which has no part in its habitual interests. A holiday in the Maldives provides a unique opportunity to experience first hand this unspoilt and paradisiacal nature which it is difficult to find elsewhere.

Two beautiful pictures of the enchanted underwater world of the Maldives. Below, a Cephalopholis miniata, a species of grouper.

THE "SECRETS" OF THE CORAL BARRIER REEF

Each of the Maldives atolls (incidentally, the English word atoll derives directly from the local term "atholhu") is encircled by a splendid coral barrier reef that is fundamental to the very existence of the islands.

What we call a reef is in fact an enormous living colony of madrepores or coral polyps, invertebrates with calcareous exoskeletons that over hundreds of thousands of years have stratified on the submerged slopes of a mountain or an extinct volcano.

While with time the landforms subside and/or are demolished by erosion and flatten to sea level, the outlying colony of coral polyps continues to grow, at a rate not less than that of the subsidence, to just below the surface of the water. It thus creates a barrier reef that delineates a lagoon around what remains of the ancient mountain or volcanic cone.

As the landform further subsides, it gradually becomes covered with sand and coral detritus and the island as such is born.

At this point, plants begin to take hold on the island soil, while the shallow, protected waters of the lagoon provide an ideal habitat for the myriad of different fish and the other marine species, like mollusks and gorgonids, that populate the marvelous submerged world so well loved by divers and snorkelers.

From the geological point of view, this fascinating environment is not completely isolated: the madrepores that created the Maldive atolls settled the crests of an ancient volcanic chain that extends for about 2000 kilometers from the Lakshadweep Islands, near the Indian subcontinent, to the Chagos Islands south of the equator.

The multicolored underwater world of the coral reefs of the Maldives.

*On these pages, the colorful world that welcomes divers just a few meters below the surface.
Right, a "Plumed Star." This and other gorgonids live in colonies attached to the steep sides of the reef and in cavities swept by underwater currents. Their beautiful colors and branching shapes make them a great attraction for divers.*

A Pterois volitans, a variety of "scorpionfish", the beautiful Nephtide coral and two "squirrelfish": these are nocturnal fish that hide in crevices in the reef during the day in order to protect themselves from the light.

On this page, a group of Lutjanus kasmira, of the Lutianidae family. To this family belong various species which are much prized for their meat. They are long-lived fish, with up to 20 years' life spans.
Right, the elegant silhouette of two colourful inhabitants of the Maldivian waters.

Two images of an adult shark.
Contrary to all expectations, the sharks in the sea round the Maldives are harmless and can be approached.

A group of Parapriachantus ransonneti: these small fish, the maximum length of which is 6 cm, tend to group together in colonies and seek protection in the crevices of the reef.

NORTH MALÉ
(KAAFU ATOLL)

The atoll of Kaafu, in its geographic entirety, is made up of two twin atolls: North Malé and South Malé. They stretch longitudinally from north to south for over 100 kilometers and include countless sand banks and islands, many of which are uninhabited. Altogether there are 44 tourist villages. Malé, the small capital of the large microcosm that is the archipelago of the Maldives, is situated in the lower part of the North Malé Atoll, where the island of Thulusdhoo, which acts as the administrative center of the atoll, and Kaashidhoo, an independent atoll over the *Five Degree Channel,* are also important. This is also the most densely populated island. An unusual custom practised by the natives here is that of "tapping" palm wine from the tree that is so abundant here and throughout the rest of the archipelago as to have become a national symbol.
In the whole archipelago, the atoll of Kaafu is where the largest numbers of tourists stay. As a consequence there are a great number of tourist villages and other structures, equipped with all types of comfort and infrastructures for rest, recreation, and sports. Among the many activities for vacationers, windsurfing and underwater fishing are probably the most popular. And with good reason, since the atoll is blessed with extraordinary, crystalline, transparent waters that host a very well developed ichthyofauna with great variety within the various species.

FARUKOLHUFUSHI
(CLUB MED FARU)

The island of Farukolhufushi stands among the tourist pearls of the North Malé Atoll, with a *Club Méditerranée* that is the second largest tourist village in the Maldives.
The buildings of the village fit harmoniously into the splendid and uncontaminated natural setting of the island. The shallow waters of the lagoon surround a dream island in an emerald green embrace.
Like in a fairy tale, the island of fine white sand is shaded by coconut palms and adorned with lush greenery. This island, because of its particular characteristics, is the perfect place for those who desire a peaceful seaside holiday—but it is also a windsurfer's heaven.

The island of Farukolhufushi from the sea.

On these pages, some views of the Club Méditerranée, with its characteristic buildings, on the island of Farukolhufushi: a romantic paradise, with bungalows caressed by the palm fronds and sparkling beaches washed by the emerald waters of the lagoon.

Club Med

Images of Vihamanaafushi: the tranquillity of Kurumba village with its visitor facilities immersed in the island's lush flora; below, a detail of the splendid bougainvilleas that color the island.

VIHAMANAAFUSHI
(KURUMBA VILLAGE)

Vihamanaafushi is one of the most visited tourist islands of the archipelago, partly because it is near Hulhule airport, which is about 3 kilometers away, but mainly because it is quite near Malé.
Numerous visitors arrive here on day trips, as do businessmen and guests of the Maldivian government who can make use of many available infrastructures (rooms for meetings, conferences, and banquets).
Kurumba Village can be reached by dhoni in just 30 minutes sailing time. It is a medium-high class tourist village, which can boast of being the first settlement of this type in the archipelago of the Maldives. Since it was founded, in 1972, this holiday village has been enlarged and refurbished several times (the work done in 1987 was particularly impressive).
At *Kurumba*—which in the native language has the curious meaning "young coconut"—holiday-makers will find international-level hotel infrastructures situated in bungalows with straw or tile roofs, restaurants, bars, cafés, a night club, a swimming pool, and a leisure centre equipped with a gym.

Here and on the following pages, the serene beauty of the island of Bodu Bandos, with its white sand beaches sloping ever so gently toward the extraordinary transparencies of the ocean waters. The luxuriant flora, enlivened by the bright colors of tropical flowers, embraces the bungalows of the village.

Left, various views of the exuberant equatorial vegetation on the island of Vihamanaafushi.

BODU BANDOS
(Bandos Island Resort)

The incomparably beautiful island of Bodu Bandos is situated north of Malé: from the airport about 8 kilometers or 45 minutes' sailing time in a characteristic dhoni.
This island, with good reason, has been described as the "capital" of the archipelago for all those keen on underwater fishing and diving in general. It seems to be a paradox, but the fortunes of this island of the Maldives have increased substantially because of the numerous sharks which live in its waters. Fortunately for all, from swimmers to experienced subs, they are whale sharks (*Rhinocadon typus*), which thanks to their small teeth feed only on plankton and small fish. In size, however, they number among the largest of the selachians and indeed of all sea fish (in fact, they can grow to 15 metres long).
Since the days when the first reckless skindivers dared to hover in front of the sharks in order to hand-feed them with small fish, Bodu Bandos has

enjoyed geat popularity among divers, obviously attracted by the well-chosen tourist maxim that touts the island as so hospitable that "even the sharks are friendly."
Given the importance of underwater sports for Bodu Bandos, a permanent medical structure is being provided and will be equipped with a hyperbaric chamber, which will function as a support facility for treatment of divers from this and other islands of the archipelago.
The tourist village, with its bungalows, refreshment, diving facilities, and an aquarium, blends harmoniously into the lovely natural setting of the island.

KUDA BANDOS

The incomparable charm of the little island of Kuda Bandos, which can be reached in a few minutes' sailing from Bodu Bandos, is enhanced by the fact that it is completely uninhabited and free of construction. It is a paradisiacal setting, where the coconut palms lean lazily over the waters of the ocean, in a picture of fairy-tale charm. In order to protect its undeniable environmental value, Kuda Bandos has been declared a nature reserve.

Another image of Bodu Bandos, where coconut palms grow right down to the water.

Kuda Bandos, famous for its equatorial vegetation, is a protected nature preserve.

BAROS

(Baros Holidays Resort)

The island of Baros lies about 15 kilometers from the airport and can be reached in an hour's sailing. The tourist village on Baros is one of the oldest in the whole archipelago, dating back to 1973. It is made up of fifty bungalows and offers its regular clients (mostly English) a good restaurant and Bavarian instructors at the diving school.

Thanks to the crystalline transparency of the waters, it is extremely easy to spot marine fauna around the island of Baros.

The magical charms of the island of Ihuru, a paradise for holiday makers in search of limpid waters with amazing reflections, unpolluted nature, and luxuriant flora. Underwater fishers can test their ability at the drop-off called "The Wall," an ideal underwater training ground for diving buffs.
These pictures show lush coconut palms growing right to the waterline, the island seen from a characteristic dhoni, an aerial view of Ihuru, and a partial view of the tourist village.

IHURU

(IHURU ANGSANA TOURIST RESORT)

This minute little oval-shaped island is one of the most prized by photographers and divers. It is, in fact, one of the most striking and charming islands in the whole archipelago. For reasons of space (only 74 guests can stay in the village) and the limited availability of fresh water—soon to be obviated by a desalination plant—Ihuru offers an ideal setting, free from annoying crowds.
The tourist "discovery" of the island dates back to 1978, when the attractive village, made up of rustic bungalows with straw-covered roofs, was constructed here. Before this Ihuru was a completely uninhabited island where only chance fishermen and people looking for coconuts stopped. Because it is very small it is possible to walk round the whole perimeter in just a quarter of an hour.

These photographs, taken on Vabbinfaru, illustrate the general color scheme of the islands in the Maldives archipelago: the green of the land, the white of the beaches, the turquoise of the shallow waters, and the intense blue of the ocean deeps.

VABBINFARU

(BANYAN TREE MALDIVES)

Vabbinfaru is situated northwest of Hulhule airport, near the island of Ihuru, and it also has a tourist village of relatively small size. The guests are housed in picturesque circular-plan bungalows, with straw roofs, which blend in well with the characteristics of the island scenery.

Holiday-makers (who are mostly Italian, French, and Australian) are able to practice various sports here: waterskiing, windsurfing, underwater fishing, and diving, for which there are also courses available.

Lastly, numerous trips to the islands of the North Malé atoll (Boduhithi, Giraavaru, Himmafushi, Thulhaagiri) are offered, even if many guests prefer enjoying a totally relaxing holiday, made up solely of sun, sand, and sea.

Here and on the following pages, different aspects of Boduhithi. Seen from above and from the sea, all the wild splendor of an equatorial island that has rightly earned the name of "Island of Coral."

BODUHITHI

(Boduhithi Coral Island)

Seen from the plane, the island of Boduhithi looks like a dark green spot, surrounded by a vaguely sickle-shaped emerald-green lagoon, around which the abyssal depths of the ocean spread out.
Situated about 30 kilometers northwest of the airport, this island can be reached in about three quarters of an hour by the fast boat. But for those who prefer an enjoyable sail through the marvelous island scenery of the North Malé atoll, it is much more advisable to use the characteristic dhoni which, although slower, allows time to better appreciate the nature of the islands and the enchanting beauty of the lagoons and coral formations.
Also known as *Coral Island*, Boduhithi is one of the favourite destinations of Italian tourists. Accommodation is available in a large number of huts with straw roofs.
In addition to the usual recreational activities centering on the extraordinarily rich and unpolluted marine environment, the island also offers wide beaches of extremely fine white sand. The gentle sloping of the sand towards the ocean allows sufficiently safe and relaxed bathing even for less experienced swimmers or families with small children. There are many coconut palms and therefore an abundance of the delicious fruits; however, they must be specially requested from the staff in charge and never picked directly from the plant. The palms, in fact, although leased to the company which manages the tourist villages, are, like the rest of the natural environment, the property of the Government of the Maldives.

An interesting aerial view of the island of Thulusdhoo, an excellent example of the general conformation of the islands of the archipelago generated by the growing corals. Located northeast of the Hulhule airport, Thulusdhoo has not yet been exploited for installing vacation village facilities. The island, home to a typical fishing village, has preserved intact its character as an equatorial island. The most adventurous of tourists will be able to find accommodations on these islands; although a world away from the comforts and services of the tourist resorts, the fishermen's islands offer the interesting opportunity to live for awhile in direct contact with the islanders and their customs and culture.

A suggestive image of Dhiffushi, another island not yet exploited by the tourist industry.

*A view of a fishing village,
with its small homes built of coral rock,
and the omnipresent coconut palm,
the national tree of the Maldives, on the beach.*

HIMMAFUSHI

In the tourist lexicon of the Maldives, Himmafushi is known as a "fishermen's island." Numerous tourist villages on the nearby islands organize trips to these islands give vacationers a taste of traditional life in the archipelago and above all its ancient economic activity: fishing.
It is certainly an interesting experience to personally watch the fishermen engaged in repairing their boats or unloading their catch by hand and transporting the fish by the most rudimentary means, when they return from fishing.
The island, unlike many other sister islands in the archipelago, has no tourist developments and has kept its own distinctive character.

On this and the next page, images of Kanifinolhu with its characteristic tourist facilities, guest accommodations, and the quiet beach fringed with palms.

An enormous equatorial tree on the island of Kanifinolhu.

KANIFINOLHU

(CLUB MED KANI)

Less than 20 kilometers separate the Huhule International Airport from this island to the north, but nevertheless Kanifinolhu seems to belong to another world. A world in which Nature dipped into her palette of colors and laid down wide brushstrokes of deep green to create this jewel of the Indian Ocean; she then set her creation in a candid bezel of coral beaches and wrapped it all in the transparent turquoise of the lagoon. In the shade of the palms inclined by the prevailing winds, and immersed in exuberant tropical vegetation, the *Club Méditerranée* greets its guests with a variety of accommodations—and sports and entertainment suitable for any vacation palate.

KUDAHITHI

(KUDAHITI TOURIST RESORT)

Not far from Boduhithi, this island is situated 28 kilometers north-west of Hulhule airport and can be reached in around 45 minutes' sailing (fast boat). The tourist village is numbered among those of the high-luxury class and is made up exclusively of a few cottages which bear distinctive names (*Captain's Cabin, Maldivian Apartment, Safari Lodge, Sheik's Cottage, The King, The Rehendi*). Here it is possible to enjoy a dream holiday in an intimate environment on an island where, rather than the usual recreational activities of the archipelago, the *dolce far niente* is the rule. Kudahithi is, in fact, the ideal place for whoever needs a restorative after stress, amply provided by spending a holiday in close contact with the wild and enchanting equatorial environment.

An aerial view of the island of Kudahithi and a detail of its beach, with the cottages set in the green of the equatorial vegetation.

Striking views of the island of Thulhaagiri: a view from the boat, a detail of the tourist village set in the midst of dense vegetation, bungalows overlooking the beach, and an exemple of the luxuriant island flora.

THULHAAGIRI

(THULHAAGIRI ISLAND RESORT)

The island of Thulhaagiri can be easily reached in an hour's crossing in dhoni from the airport, 11 kilometers away. The tourist village is managed by a French company and most of the vacationers and guests who come here to spend their holidays are also French.
As on many sister islands of the vast Maldivian archipelago, courses to learn diving techniques and the skills of underwater fishing are available to tourists and are, here as elsewhere, the most popular and requested activities. What situation can be better than these paradisiacal islands for whoever wishes to fully savor the hidden fascination of the depths of the sea or see fish of the most varied species and dimensions, all, however, in a chromatic range which seems to have come straight from the colors of the rainbow.

NAKACHCHAAFUSHI
(Nakatchafushi Tourist Resort)

From Hulhule airport, this island (22 kilometers to the northwest) can be reached in 90 minutes in a dhoni, which is still the most widespread means of transport in the archipelago.
The village here is mid class, even though it is provided with all the comforts normally required and offers the usual possibilities for amusement to those interested in the most varied aspects of the sea.
A characteristic feature of this island resort is the bar on a terrace that stretches out over the waters of the ocean.

Impressions of the scenery of the island of Nakachchaafushi: a vista towards the tourist village, shaded by the slender silhouettes of the coconut palms; a picture of the beach with the pier; a view towards the sea; a detail of the large park which surrounds the village.

LANKANFUSHI

(SONEVA GILI)

This island is situated about 10 kilometers north of the airport and can be reached by boat in a little less than an hour.
A tourist village, made up of bungalows with bathrooms, occupies the central part of the island.
In addition to the usual sports and beach activities, Lankanfushi offers visitors the chance to take a boat trip to Himmafushi, where a characteristic Maldivian fishing village can be visited. This opportunity, as well as being an interesting diversion, provides an immediate means of entering into contact with the people who live here, and to observe their customs and work.

Evocative images of bungalows on pilings, and a pier jutting into the Lankanfushi lagoon.

MEERUFENFUSHI

(Meeru Island Resort)

At the eastern tip of the atoll, 50 kilometers north of the international airport, Meerufenfushi ("island of sweet water") is easily reached aboard fast vessels: an hour on the sea takes the visitor to an island which is not only one of the largest in the archipelago, but also one of the most beautiful, abounding in lush vegetation, with exceptional gardens and banana groves, and many lovely secluded beaches.
The *Meeru Island Resort* (227 rooms in bungalows and water bungalows) is the ideal village for a full-relaxation vacation in a not overly formal atmosphere. Windsurfing, 5-player soccer, volleyball, catamaraning, darts, canoeing, and fishing are the sports offered by the resort, but the real attraction is the local diving center, which, with its diving school, permits anyone—from beginners to expert divers—to enjoy exciting dives at uncrowded sites along the coral barrier reef, some of which are actually reserved for the enjoyment of the resort guests alone.

Meerufenfushi: plays of light and shadow on the island's enchanting beach, and the fast vessels that guarantee connections with the capital of the Maldives.

On these pages, Meerufenfushi from different angles: the tourist and sports facilities, the exuberant natural beauties of the island, the singular restaurant with its sloping straw roof and sand floor, and the museum, which displays the gigantic remains of an ancient whale.

An aerial view of the island of Lhohifushi in the spectacular emerald-green embrace of the shoals of its lagoon. The island, which can be reached in dhoni, has a tourist village patronized by a cosmopolitan mix of visitors.

Here and on the next page, the island of Lankhanfinolhu and its resort: a paradisiacal corner of the enchanted garden that is the archipelago of the Maldives.

LANKHANFINOLHU

(PARADISE ISLAND RESORT)

Twenty minutes in a speedboat are all it takes to reach one of the most modern vacation villages in the Maldives: the *Paradise Island Resort*, which with its 260 rooms is also one of the largest. Restaurants featuring international, Italian, and Japanese cuisine cater to the guests, who come from all parts of the world. The resort also offers its guests a number of different bars, game rooms, and pools, as well as a health spa and, of course, a wide range of sports on dry land and in the water.
Shows and a discotheque enliven the evenings under the enchanting equatorial firmament.

While the placid waters of the lagoon caress the coral shoulders of Lankhanfinolhu and the palms extend their fronds almost as though to protect vacationers with their shade, an exotic bird strolls undisturbed on the beach—an unequivocal sign of how non-invasive man's presence here has been.

Paradise Island

KUDAHURAA

(Four Seasons Resort)

A well-being center for massages, beauty treatments, and relaxation therapies, a marvelous pool, three restaurants with something for every palate, an enchanting tropical garden, 106 luxury bungalows of various types—some with private pools—at the seaside or literally "on" the water, an excellent diving center. And then shops, live music, organized evenings with entertainment, a discotheque, a coffee shop. All this and more awaits the guests of the *Four Seasons Resort*, one of the most beautiful in the luxury category.

Here and on the next page, some views of scenic Kudahuraa and its resort, one of the Maldives' most beautiful and luxurious.

Left, two more images of the serenely beautiful Lankhanfinolhu.

SOUTH MALÉ
(KAAFU ATOLL)

VELASSARU

(LAGOONA BEACH)

Among the tourist islands which make up the island microcosm of the atoll of South Malé (*Kaafu Atoll*), that of Velassaru is numbered among the most famous from the vacationing point of view.
Situated about 10 kilometers southwest of Hulhule airport, it is also known by the evocative name of *Lagoona Beach* after the resort opened there in 1974. That which until relatively recently was considered as one of the 300 most exclusive hotels in the world has now been reconverted into a medium-high level tourist village.
The original development, although in close contact with the extraordinary nature of the Maldivian archipelago, was not provided with the comforts and modern communications that are today the boast of the tourist village.

The exuberant, multicolored flora that ensconces the tourist village on Velassaru, and a panorama of the island, with its bungalows on pilings.

The sparkling of the sea waters of Velassaru, framed by the dark green of the island vegetation.

The splendid swimming pool of Laguna Beach in the green embrace of the coconut palms, the real protagonists in the lush natural scenery of the Maldives.

The tourist dock on the island of Velassaru marks the divide between the shallow water of the lagoon and the deeper sea.

Windsurfers on the calm waters of Velassaru.

A prominent feature is the swimming pool, which sinuously fits into the lush exuberance of the coconut palms, which in their turn, along with the traditional straw-roofed huts, pleasantly shade the repose of guests and tourists. Windbreaks in the form of coral walls have been built in order to protect the cottages from gusts of equatorial wind.
Diving and underwater fishing enthusiasts will find this a perfect vacation spot, where they can count on the assistance of expert instructors.

The island of Vaadhoo.

On the following pages: some views of Biyaadhoo, where the exceptional transparency of the water reveals the most minute details of the sea bottom, a paradise for divers; two views of the village.

VAADHOO

(VAADHOO DIVING PARADISE)

The island of Vaadhoo lies just 8 kilometers from Hulhule airport.
Around the island are areas abounding in varieties of countless types of marine life. Those in the know class these waters as some of the best sites in the entire archipelago for diving in general and for underwater fishing.
There is a medium-high class tourist village here, patronized mainly by European and Japanese tourists. Due to the fact that it is situated on the edge of the deep channel which separates the atoll of South Malé from that of North Malé, the island is also known in no uncertain terms as the epitome of the Maldives "diving paradise."

BIYAADHOO

(BIYAADHOO ISLAND RESORT)

This island, situated 28 kilometers southwest of the airport, can be reached by boat in about two and a half hours. Alternatives for more impatient tourists are provided by fast boat and helicopter.
The tourist village here has the distinction of being made up of two-story buildings, extremely rare in the Maldives. Among the sports and recreational activities, scuba diving and underwater fishing take the lead. The waters around Biyaadhoo, like those around the nearby Viligilivaru, are extraordinarily crystalline and transparent and offer numerous renowned places for enjoying of these sports. Water-skiing and windsurfing are alternatives with large followings.

These pictures document the serene beauty of Viligilivaru, from the charm of its sea to the magic of its sandy shores and the exotic vitality of its flowers and plants.
The island is also a well-known paradise for divers, as the wet-suits hung out to dry in the village would suggest.

VILIGILIVARU
(VILIVARU ISLAND RESORT)

The island of Viligilivaru is closely linked, not only from a geographical point of view, with the nearby Biyaadhoo, of which it may be said to be the "younger sister."
The transport and communications systems of the twin islands are controlled by a single company, which also manages the tourist villages and their restaurants and bars. This translates into a series of advantages for the guests: for example, rumor has it that the food at the Viligilivaru and Biyadhoo resorts is the best in the entire archipelago!
The island of Viligilivaru offers exceptional natural surroundings to holiday-makers, enhanced by the amazing transparency of its waters and the magic of its sandy shores. It is rich in charming secluded places, where the white madreporic sand beaches slope imperceptibly into the warm and enchanting emerald-green waters of the ocean—a true Eden for divers and hunters of marine prey—while the green fronds of the coconut palms guarantee a shady haven for bathers who prefer idling away their vacation hours.

MAHAANA ELHI HURAA

(Rihiveli Beach Resort)

Of the innumerable pearls in the precious necklace of the South Malé Atoll, Mahaana Elhi Huraa is the southernmost of all. The island is in fact some 40 kilometers from the Hulhule airport.

Like those of the great majority of the atoll's islands, the tourist village of the paradisiacal Mahaana Elhi Huraa caters to a widely-varied international clientele. And just as many islands seem to attract predominantly visitors of one or another nationality, *Rihiveli Beach*'s guests are in the main Australians.

In fact, in many areas the natural features are still in their wild state, untouched by development and in no way disturbed or altered by the tourists who visit the island, despite their great numbers.

In addition to the "usual" sea-related sports, sunbathing, and swimming, the resort also offers its

Two views of the wonderful sandy beach on Mahaana Elhi Huraa.

Characteristic dhonis on the lagoon.

A strange construction, its roof built around a dhoni prow, rises out of the lagoon on pilings.

Striking aspects of the lagoon microcosm of Mahaana Elhi Huraa, with its splendid sandy shores and magnificent coconut palms.

A characteristic village bungalow, and the interior of a tourist bungalow.

guests the opportunity to take rides aboard the characteristic dhonis, and even two-day mini-cruises. Four-passenger boats escort visitors around the whole atoll to explore the beauties of the sea and the island.

The restaurant is a distinctive feature of the *Rihiveli Beach Resort* (which is made up of almost fifty bungalows) as it is charmingly situated outdoors, facing the lagoon.

Holiday-makers looking for a break from sedentary sunbathing might want to ford the lagoon on foot to explore the small uninhabited islands "of the Rising Sun" and "of the Birds," where the unpolluted nature of these islands can be seen at its best.

OLHUVELI
(Olhuveli View Hotel)

This island, situated 39 kilometers from the airport, has a tourist village patronized mainly by Japanese and Italian vacationers. At low tide it is possible to ford the lagoon to reach a nearby island.

BODUFINOLHU
(Fun Island Resort)

"Fun Island" (38 kilometers from the airport), stands out because of the numerous recreational and sports activities offered to the guests of the village. At low tide two small uninhabited islands can be reached on foot.

The tourist village of Olhuveli seen from the lagoon.

The crystalline turquoise of the waters encircling the islands is an irresistible invitation to explore its underwater marvels, even for vacationers who intended only to lazily enjoy the shade of the palms.

VELIGANDU HURAA BODU HURAA DHIGUFINOLHU

(Palm Tree Island Resort)

Just a little over 30 kilometers from the airport, three drops of emerald green and white in a turquoise lagoon make up a single resort, *Palm Tree Island*. The islets are linked by footbridges for strolls, as fascinating as they may seem incredible, over the placid waters of the lagoon. The unusual layout of the resort makes a stay on any of the three islets a unique experience, since of course guests are free to roam from onea village to another to participate in the various sports activities, or to dine at a different restaurant, and may want to stop for a drink at the charming bar set on pilings in the middle of the lagoon, at the crossroads of the resort's unusual "road system" over the water. A fourth islet (Bushi, also linked to the footbridge system) is reserved for the staff quarters and all the service structures (like the desalinating plant)—but also hosts the resort's diving center.

Here and on the preceding pages, the singular images that greet the eyes of guests at the Palm Tree Island Resort, which covers three green islands (plus a fourth for service facilities). Suspended walkways link the islands to permit guests to take long—and quite unusual—strolls over the water.

Visions of paradise and symbolic images of this extraordinary archipelago: Makunufushi and its resort.

Left, two enchanting views of the island of Dhigufinolhu.

MAKUNUFUSHI
(COCOA BEACH & SPA)

The small resort on this island—enchanted like all the others in the archipelago—offers the visitor the unique opportunity to stay in a dhoni, the traditional Maldivian boat. A number of these vessels, at anchor in the lagoon, have been transformed into comfortable vacation suites.

KANDOOMAFUSHI

(Kandooma Resort)

Thanks to its price policy, the *Kandooma Resort* has attained great popularity among the many Maldivian tourist villages. It is in fact one of the less expensive on the entire archipelago, with rooms that are plain but comfortable and informal bars that serve drinks at affordable prices. The resort attracts a type of clientele interested mostly in diving, snorkeling, and related activities, for whom it organizes daily excursions to interesting portions of the reef and diving in the various reef channels (*kandu* in the Maldivian language) not far from the island, all at more than reasonable prices. Diving sites like the Guraidhoo Kandu Protected Marine Area make this a true paradise for underwater enthusiasts.

Sought out by diving enthusiasts for the characteristics of its underwater sites, the island of Kandoomafushi offers excellent accommodations for vacationers.

VAAVU ATOLL
(FELIDHU ATOLL)

The atoll of Vaavu, situated 67 kilometers south of Malé, is made up of 24 islands, of which only five are inhabited.
Two tourist villages are to be found here. The administrative center of the atoll is Felidhoo. The population of this atoll adds up altogether to slightly fewer than 1,700 persons.
From an administrative point of view, the atoll also includes that of Vattaru.
In addition to the administrative center and the tourist islands of Alimatha and Dhiggiri, the islands of Keyodhoo and Rakeedhoo, which are among the larger ones, must be mentioned.

ALIMATHA

(Alimatha Aquatic Resort)

The island of Alimatha is situated 61 kilometers south of Hulhule airport. The crossing to the island is usually by fast boat and takes about 90 minutes. There is a medium-level tourist village here. The visitors who stay here are predominantly Italian, mainly people who practice underwater fishing and those keen on diving in general. The waters and the marine recesses of Alimatha are particularly suitable for these sports. A trip to the nearby tourist island of Dhiggiri is another popular pastime among vacationers on Alimatha.

The island of Alimatha and the tourist village seen from the boat.

Bottom, a view of the pier on the island of Alimatha with one of the boats that guarantee connections with the other islands, and a windsurfer in shade of coconut palms with the magical sea of the Maldives in the background.

A marvelous backlit picture of the island of Alimatha.

INDEX

THE WONDERFUL WORLD OF THE MALDIVES
NORTH MALÉ - SOUTH MALÉ - VAAVU

Project and editorial concept: Casa Editrice Bonechi
Editorial management: Serena de Leonardis
Picture research: Giovanna Magi
Graphic design and cover: Manuela Ranfagni
Layout: Sauro Giampaia
Editing: Rita Bianucci, Maurizio Morelli
English translation by Kate Parenti *with additional translations by* Paula Boomsliter

Texts by Rita Bianucci, Maurizio Morelli, Giuliano Valdes - Editing Studio, Pisa
Introduction by Riccardo Mazzanti
Text on page 54 by Giuseppe D'Amato
Maps by Stefano Benini

Printed in Italy by Centro Stampa Editoriale Bonechi.

The photographs are property of the Casa Editrice Bonechi photographic archives and were taken by Paolo Giambone *except for the following: p. 55, 58 top, 61 top, 62, 63, photos by* Marco Eletti*; p. 8, 56, 57 photos by* Andrea Ghisotti.

For the photographs with no identified source, the publisher would be pleased to include the appropriate acknowledgements in any subseguent edition.

ISBN 88-476-1175-X

***